A model of
Collaborative Society

D. Palix
2016

To my lovely wife and children, family and friends

Thank you. Without your support, patience and remarks, I would never have given shape to this most comforting idea.

Site web : www.collaborative-society.org

Copyright © 2016 by D. Palix.

ISBN < 978-1-326-53067-9>

TABLE OF CONTENTS

New democratic principles

Analysis

The political and economic systems in the Western world seem now well established. Representative democracy and liberal model have been the cause of constant progress and relative social peace within countries that have adopted them, and even if they are not perfect, few people really consider deep changes.

Yet, it seems wise to take a critical look on these systems, see what makes their strengths and weaknesses, and imagine other significantly different models.

Although such changes are rare, and may seem utopian, having a new and really more satisfactory model, which can impose itself over time, is essential.

It is true that any major change is a risk, particularly at the scale of a country or civilization, and we have seen in recent decades the bitter failure of other attractive models, such as the communist one. Many will prefer improving the existing system little by little, or experiment local solutions.

Even though all this is clearly valuable, we need at some point to come up with a new system that is viable at a wide scale.

To achieve this, we'll have to go as far as elaborating **new democratic principles**, an essential approach to change our institutions thoroughly, and ultimately our society and our civilization.

As a first step, let's recall the **definition of the democratic model**: a model of government "by the people, for the people". It seduces every citizen because it makes us feel that we collectively have control of our destiny. Unfortunately, we are far from the expected ideal. Worse, we have rarely been feeling so powerless, unable to really influence the course of events.

On the **political** side, the record abstention rate is quite indicative of this fact, citizens being tired of non-held promises, the influence of lobbies, and the immense gap between themselves and politicians. A major drawback of the system lies on minority no longer being represented once the elections are over. Even the elected majority also just endures the system for the duration of the mandates. Governments themselves have a limited control over things, as their budget, thus their policy, is so dependent on the efficiency of the economic system, as a result of globalization of the economy.

Regarding the **economic** system, we appreciate the strength of the liberal model: dynamism, innovation, efficiency, motivation of economic actors… However, the activity is mostly profit-driven, and customers' influence on the system is quite indirect and minor. Even worse, this model requires considerable freedoms in the economic practices, source of chaotic phases and manifold abuses.

It also has social consequences, as unemployed people are numerous and inequalities are huge. And it loses in efficiency, being overly focused on **competition** and not enough offering opportunities for **collaboration** between all its actors.

Another shortcoming of the current model of society is its very **hierarchical organization**, leading to indisputable positions of power and considerable opacity in all areas. It's an issue because any position of absolute power opens a loophole in which the human soul rushes easily, often leading to abuse of power, and to the satisfaction of personal or private interest at the expense of many.

The **reduced control and transparency**, especially on financial flows, also open the door to organized crime, with all the social consequences that we know.

Among the various proposals aiming at improving society, some suggest to increase the participation of the citizens in the decision-making process. But a purely **participative model**, where all persons interested in a topic take decisions by direct democracy, each contributing in the decision by one voice, is illusory. Such a model is valid in limited cases, but would be too cumbersome to implement at a wide scale. It also denies that the decision-making process, the capacity to endorse a solution to a problem requires knowledge and skills that we cannot ask everyone to master. A decision-maker is a visionary, someone whose talent is to anticipate the effects of each possible solution, in order to retain the best one.

Eventually, this short analysis defines a **very clear orientation** for the new model we want to elaborate:

- It must give a thorough control to the citizens, while keeping a real dynamism.

- It must also minimize the positions of absolute power, while keeping decision-maker positions.

- It must rely on both notions of competition and collaboration, and maximize transparency.

- Finally, this model is useful if it is not just a utopia, i.e. its implementation does not seem unrealistic and can even be experimented in some ways.

Propositions

So, how shall we take into account these guidelines, what are the key ideas on which to build a new model of society?

Clearly we need to modify the current decision-making processes fundamentally. We need in fact to give birth to a new **decision-making model**, i.e. answer the following questions:
- Who sets the objectives and associated means and how?
- Who takes decisions and how?
- How do the people in charge of this evolve over time?

The model that I propose relies on the following ideas. These should be perceived as new democratic principles:

Let people express themselves on the type of society desired, through well designed forms. The democratic synthesis of the results sets the precise objectives and associated means for each area of activity.
But let decision-makers choose in an autonomous manner the final solutions to achieve these goals.

This principle has an immediate consequence: we no longer want decision-makers who strive to achieve their own vision of society or strive for they own personal benefit. We want to grant power to those decision-makers who are able to fulfill at best the objectives set by citizens.

This is achieved through the following principle:

Let's make sure to have multiple decision-makers per area of activity, grant some decision-making power to each decision-maker, and adjust the power of all decision-makers over time depending on their respective results. These are evaluated per area as the ability to achieve the objectives defined by citizens.

These are already big changes, but we need to add one more, another principle that will guarantee an efficient link between citizens and decision-makers:

In each area, citizens' representatives tune the objectives and associated means, oversee the decision-making process, and can support new decision-makers. They are chosen by area, randomly, among the volunteers with a good knowledge of the area, and are renewed frequently. They take their decisions through an improved direct democracy process.

Ultimately it is a model where everyone finds their logical place:
- **Citizens** express themselves relatively to what they can legitimately and practically speak on: what they feel about current society, the frustrations and issues they face, their wishes and values, all in all the **social and economic framework** that will orient all decisions.
- But decisions are made by competent **decision-makers**, that is to say people whose skill is to take decisions, who have a talent for it. They are also focused per area, accumulating knowledge that let them take good decisions.

- The **representatives** have limited power but a crucial role. They embody the link between the citizens and the decision-makers, an effective link due to their knowledge of the area.

Eventually, what defines best this model is this balance between all people involved, with representatives fully embodying the collaborative spirit of the model. This model is thus called a "**collaborative**" model.

Development

These new principles establish a **paradigm shift**, affecting society in its fundamental aspects.

But there is much to build on top of them: we now need to define **new institutions** giving shape to a "**collaborative society**". Doing so is essential to guarantee that these principles are viable.

In the next chapter, I will thus first give an overview of this new model of society.

I will then aim at delivering the appropriate details embodying this vision, without getting lost in a too developed essay. We will have to see in particular how to let citizens express themselves on the type of society they desire, what the decision-making power allocated to decision-makers corresponds to, and what the evaluation process relies on.

Finally, such a change in society may seem utopian on paper. I will thus conclude by paying attention to how such a model can take shape for real. I will highlight the fact that even if the intentions are to depart noticeably from the existing situation, structures at the base remain similar. Citizens take control of their destiny by taking control of means of production, financial flows and decision-making processes. And these changes, although ambitious, are realistic, with possible experiments in some public services.

Diagrams

Let's conclude this first chapter by two diagrams.

The first diagram indicates, for various models of society:
- the level of control exercised by the citizens,
- and the skill level required for decision-makers.

It highlights the fact that the proposed collaborative model offers both a high level of control exercised by citizens, and highly skilled decision-makers.

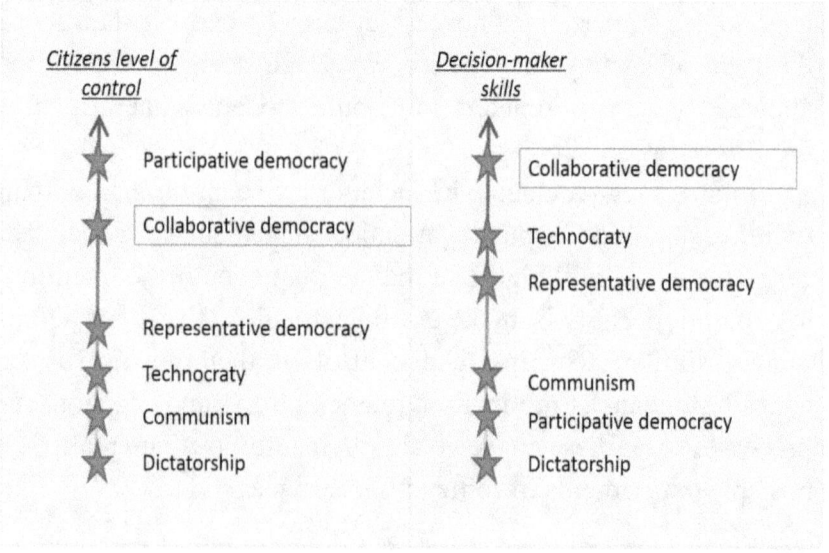

The second one illustrates the *collaborative decision-making model* as a whole.

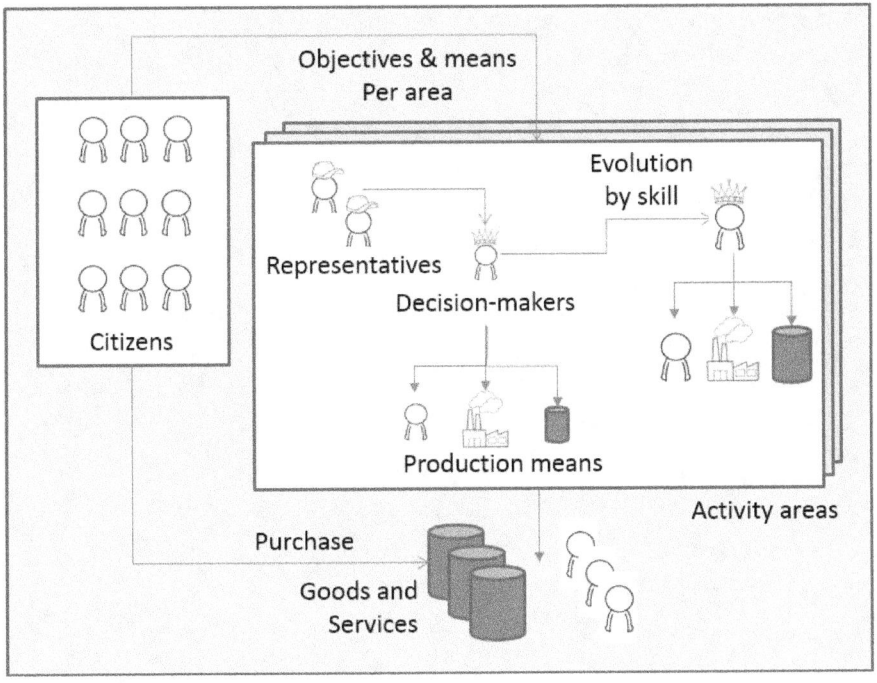

-   **Objectives & means**: defined per area, by citizens, through direct democratic process, and detailed by representatives, chosen randomly.
-   **Decisions**: production mandates established by autonomous decision-makers.
-   **Decision-makers coming into power and evolution**: decision-makers come to power essentially (but not only) by representatives. Their power, initially low, evolves according to their capacity to achieve objectives better than their direct competitors.

A new vision of society

Now let's use our imagination, while reviewing together this new model of society through a synthetic vision spread on a few pages. An exercise which could prove a little difficult because the details describing each part will come afterwards, in the following chapter; also it's certainly not easy to concretely perceive a society based on radically different rules, and understand how all aspects work together.

Let's proceed logically, developing each of the new democratic principles one after the other, and while doing so, put in light how this affects our institutions.

The first pane of the proposed model is to **let citizens define the type of society they want to live in,** through a direct democracy process. In other words, the citizens do not vote for a person or a party but raise key information that will then define the social and economic framework guiding all decision-making.

It consists in sharing one's opinions with respect to substantive issues that affect everyone. By sharing one's values and specifying how we feel about all aspects of our current society, it's possible to define in which direction we want collectively to make our society evolve, in all areas.

These topics are elaborated by representatives of the citizens in each area. The answers can be changed at any time, and are regularly (in example annually) summarized and taken into account.

This approach requires that we specify how we give decision-makers the means to achieve the goals set by citizens, i.e. really steer human activities in all areas.

There is no other choice but to **change all financial flows**, thus effectively replacing the public model (based on taxes) and the private one (based on sales revenue). The idea is to switch to a logic of overall investment, considering that each year an **overall budget** (fixed and arbitrary) is available and must be invested in all the means of production: human (wages) and material (annual rental cost of existing infrastructure, and rights to use natural resources).

Taking into account the framework defined by citizens, the overall budget can be broken out per area of activity, so that decision-makers in each area have the means to finance related activities.

To complete the decision-making model further, we now have to detail the second pane of the proposed model: in each economic and social area, we want to grant decision-makers with some **decision-making power**, and update this power depending on their skill, i.e. their efficiency.

Two decision-making processes are possible, each for a specific context.

The first decision-making process, called "**competitive**", is used when multiple solutions can be implemented in a given area of activity. This model will be applied very broadly, including all areas corresponding presently to the private economy, where competition is quite common.

The budget defined for an area is split among the decision-makers of this area, depending on their respective power. They can then invest it in a fully autonomous way, their goal being to target the most relevant activities, delivering production mandates to economic structures, or adjusting these when appropriate.

We guarantee the system's efficiency by adjusting the economic power of each decision-maker based on his or her results: these are compared with the results of all other decision-makers of the same area; we then let the most efficient decision-makers progress in power.

Another decision-making process, called "**concerted**", heavier to implement, must be applied when we cannot have multiple solutions, or when the stakes are high. For example, to define laws or standards, or to manage a specific resource, such as a high value tourist site, a worldwide sports competition...

We need a mechanism that allows us to select a solution among all those proposed by the various decision-makers involved, a mechanism that is better than a simple majority vote, but instead takes into account the skill of each decision-maker. Finally, this mechanism must allow reassessment of this skill in order to advance the best ones.

We will detail the precise mechanism used in the next chapter, but in a nutshell, let's say that the idea is to ask each decision-maker involved to evaluate by anticipation the effect of each proposed solution, relatively to the wishes expressed by the citizens. These values are weighted by the decision-making power of each decision-maker. The solution with the most overall support is applied.

This decision-making process comes with an evaluation process that encourages each decision-maker to position himself or herself on *each* solution in the fairest possible manner, rather than support only his or her own: indeed, the power of each decision-maker is re-evaluated based on the measured difference between the anticipated effect and the observed effect of the agreed solution. This process helps maintain and grow up the most skilled decision-makers, while less efficient ones have diminished power.

It avoids the too conventional way of doing politics, based on very static parties, and a very hierarchical state, centered on key personalities. It also ensures that the final decisions are those that take into account all citizens, satisfying each one in a balanced manner. Indeed, these solutions have the maximum positive effect, thus decision-makers that positively support these solutions are therefore more likely to progress than others, eventually changing behaviors in depth. All in all, it's a much better process than the classic process based on majority, or a hierarchical organization with one single decision-maker.

This process being however heavier to implement, we will try to increase the **competitive situations**, in order to favor the simplest process. We can achieve this goal by **limiting the size of economic structures**: instead of heavy structures, powerful but static, we build on a network of dynamic light autonomous structures, both in competition and in synergy, and frequent re-composition.

Note also that through the information reported by the citizens, we will specify per area a budget dedicated to **innovation** and one dedicated to **training**, ensuring a real dynamic system.

As previously mentioned, economic activity being the result of an automatic and regular investment of the entire workforce, we do not seek to obtain through sales a flow of money that will be reinvested in the economy. However, we have to define **a mechanism to share access to goods and services** between all citizens in an efficient way.

The way we proceed is simply to let the price of every good and service be conditioned by a single aspect: its scarcity, without having a minimum value. It thus evolves according to supply and demand, with two goals in mind: for goods we aim at managing the stock decrease regularly, and for services we aim at using them to almost full load.

A consequence of this approach is that all digital assets (particularly the fruit of R & D), whose offer is virtually unlimited once produced, will be free of use. It thus **enhances the effectiveness of the system**, the synergy between professionals. To emphasize this, and also to strengthen control by citizens, we will also maximize the **transparency** of all professional practices and information. This approach is made possible by the disappearance of the private economic sphere.

The **wages of the workers**, like the usage cost of natural resources and the rental cost of existing infrastructures, are also the result of supply and demand, without minima (or only a small one). This approach allows a dynamic labor market, assesses training needs, and pushes everyone to target jobs with a high demand and to strive for excellence.

In this context, the economic power of a decision-maker is finally a "scarcity" budget, giving every decision-maker the power to operate some of the means of production. We thus have a scarcity-based economy, where all notions are expressed directly and only in terms of scarcity. It guarantees that all means of production are used, and unemployment reduced.

The above approach is valid only if we put in place mechanisms of **solidarity**, guaranteeing a minimum income to everyone, via mechanisms based on basic income and rebalancing of high incomes toward the more modest ones.

Conversely, individual **enrichment** opportunities are possible through high incomes and bonuses. In a way, we can say that all means of production are owned by the community but are made available to all workers, who can gain a personal profit from them according to their results.

Eventually, **enrichment and solidarity mechanisms** are controlled by the citizens. This is done, as part of the framework definition, by letting citizens democratically define the type of society they desire: a very egalitarian society or a society where individual skills are valued financially, even though this may generate social tensions. This input will eventually be used to define all the corresponding parameters: bonuses, basic universal income, rebalancing parameters, limits on inheritance... We will however remove any speculative activity, uncontrollable by nature.

Let's conclude by speaking of the **citizens' representatives**. Two levels of representatives are needed in every area.

The first level consists of all non-paid volunteers, under the condition they have some good knowledge of the area. Their main role is to participate in surveys created for the area. These surveys will in example be done to clarify the framework (specifying how the budget should be broken out with a higher granularity, and summarizing the main issues of the area) or to allow assessment of decisions taken.

A fraction of the representatives of the first level, randomly selected among those who proved to be the most active ones and showed advanced knowledge of the domain, will have a more active role and earn a salary. Their goal is to follow up the area closely and take decisions relative to the decision-making process in order to ensure its effectiveness. It includes also granting power to new decision-makers, and be privileged interlocutors for all of them, providing appropriate details to help them take good decisions. In this sense, they fully embody the collaborative spirit of the model. They operate through an improved direct democracy mode, that we'll detail later on. They are renewed regularly (in example every three years).

System details

Let's now complement this overview with some key details.

The goal is not to expose all the details but only those who describe the model well enough for us to apprehend it quite tangibly. Through them, we want to get a concrete and fairly complete vision. It should also help make sure the previous propositions and the underlying intentions seem viable.

Framework definition

Framework overview

As described previously, the first step of the new decision-making process is to **let citizens define the type of society they want to live in,** through a direct democracy process.

Through appropriate forms, democratically summarized once per year (in example), it defines a clear objective given to decision-makers, a goal to achieve through their decisions. We can see it as an economic and social framework.

It's impossible to describe here the precise forms to be used. It will be the representatives' work to elaborate them, and make them evolve over time. But let's mention some key aspects.

For sure, the forms should allow people to share their values and opinions on key issues that are being debated among citizens. Some general question may appear such as "how would you feel in a society that authorizes death penalty". The number of questions may be a bit long but most will not evolve over time. Furthermore, citizens may change position on a topic but that won't occur frequently. So only the new questions will really require some time every year.

It's important to note that these questions have to be written in a way that corresponding answers don't automatically define a solution, but only a framework. In the example above, we don't ask "Should society authorize death penalty?" but "How do you feel about death penalty?". It's totally different, because the first question is sort of a referendum that leads to a decision (i.e. participative democracy), whereas the second one is only a piece of information inside a more general framework, that decision-makers shall apprehend as a whole to take their decisions.

The framework should obviously contain some financial aspects.

As mentioned before, the overall economy (in the sense "all human activities whose result is made available to others") is based on an overall budget, that is fixed and arbitrary (thus ending any notion of inflation). Through offer and demand mechanism, it enables full usage of all means of production: the entire available labor force (as salaries) but also all natural raw materials, available goods and existing infrastructures.

Through appropriate forms, citizens' feedback should enable us to break out the overall budget per area.

Other financial aspects will have to be defined as well, also through appropriate forms, such as solidarity and enrichment settings. These can be numerous but include at least:

- The share of the budget paid in bonuses to the most skilled people or teams
- The limits of transmission from an inheritance
- Parameters related to base income and income rebalancing, adjusting the final income based on earned wages and

probably other parameters like age, situation… See the section on wages & incomes further.
- The amount levied in insurance, and the activation parameters of the fees covered by such insurance (goods repair, health …).

Budget breakout per area

Let's go into more details on how we could poll people in order to define budget breakout per area of activity. The idea is to poll people about how they feel regarding each area that impact them directly, using in example a scale of predefined values, such as "are you very satisfied, satisfied, only a little satisfied, not at all satisfied?". This information is then converted into usable numerical value and the final results are summarized in a democratic manner (that is to say by working out the average value).

Areas that meet the most frustrations should have an increased budget, while the others will have a diminished budget. We thus proceed by limited updates every year so that the investment made in each area of activity eventually corresponds to what is really wanted.

Let's note that this democratic process somehow comes down to giving every citizen a fixed share of this overall budget and letting him or her invest it as he or she wishes, which is very logic: *I agree to offer my work to the community on condition that I can demand in return that others work according to my wishes.*

The resulting goods or services in each area are obviously available to all; as a consequence, everyone is encouraged to express themselves honestly on their perception of current society, as failing to do so will result in having a too limited offer compared to the demand in some area.

To facilitate the feedback, it seems wise to probe citizens through several nested levels, from macro to elementary area of activity. People can provide feedback at the macro level only or go deep only on some areas, or all, as they wish. The following paragraphs give an example of budget break out.

Detailed budget: first level

The first level is very simple; it leads to break out the budget in two:
- The part that corresponds to all common spending, that everyone will automatically benefit
- The part aimed at activities whose finality is goods and services that have to be shared between all, i.e. have to be purchased.

This split will thus have a major impact on the entire economy, thus society.

Detailed budget: second level

The second level means breaking out the budget in a number of budget items, each corresponding to a major area of activity. Here again, the final budget decided in each area will steer society in one direction or another, so the way the list is built (and the corresponding form is done) is crucial.

The next paragraph is a proposal for a list of topics on which we could poll citizens.

<u>For common spending:</u>

- **Safety**: these are all expenses done to avoid unexpected issues. It therefore includes policemen, firefighters, justice, the prison system, the army... but also all investments made to secure living and working.

- **Environment:** preserve the environment at a wide scale, or restore it, fight against global pollution and global warming...

- **Resource usage reduction:** reduce the use of resources in the solutions already at work, and also in future solutions.

- **Global services**: all services potentially useful to everyone. Includes especially all activities related to establishing new laws.

- **Global & Local administration:** all administrative services aimed directly at citizens

- **Digital content**: any digital production is free of rights, and so this area of activity is part of this common spending section. We'll distinguish for sure:

  o Useful content: any digital tool, data or piece of information that could help anyone in his day to day life.
  o Entertainment and cultural digital content

- **Fundamental research**: Though this activity impacts us in a very indirect way, we must have the possibility to express ourselves relative to the effort we want to spend on it.

- **Professional hardship reduction**: this topic will determine the budget we want to invest to improve work condition, i.e. reduce occupational hardship for the most painful jobs.

For goods & services that have to be shared (thus purchased):

- **Training**: The training activity as a whole, for children and adults.

- **Health & Repair**: this topic corresponds to a wide area of activities, all related to fixing unexpected issues, or compensate these.

- **Global production of goods**: all goods potentially shippable to anywhere in the world

- **Global services to individual people**: all other activities offering a service aimed at individual people, and that anybody can benefit, such as those related to transport or tourism.

- **Local expenses (infrastructures & operational costs)**, these correspond to local activities, offering goods or services to a local population (living at proximity). Includes all shops.

Detailed budget: extra levels

Once the previous budget items are known, another level of polling is possible in order to specify more precisely how some of these budget items shall be used. One could also imagine still one more level in some areas. The only requirement is to poll citizens regarding whole areas of activity, or specific issues (which usually is the same), and not on specific solutions.

It's up to everyone to decide how far they want to spend time on this, knowing that representatives will, in all cases, do this detailed work.

It's also important to know in which direction the allocated budget in an area of activity is to be used. We should poll citizens about this, with standard answers available, such as "*prices of a specific good or service are too high*" or "*current solutions in an area are not well adapted or non-existent*".

This will steer the activity of the area in one direction or another. For example, to reduce production costs (and thus produce more for the same total cost, reducing eventually scarcity, so the price). Or to provide goods or services that match needs better. This will determine the budget in each area that shall be allocated to **innovations (applied research), new infrastructures, or modernization or maintenance** of existing ones.

Key points of the budget approach

The mechanism described above really allows citizens to steer all human activities, and therefore the whole society, in a specific direction, such as:

- More or less **egalitarian** (through "common spending", "health and repair", "solidarity and personal enrichment settings", and "professional hardship"). Everything is possible: we can calibrate the parameters regarding these topics on the current model, or increase inequalities, or create a fully egalitarian world, where all incomes are identical. Eventually this choice is made by the citizens in a very democratic manner. See the section on wages and incomes for more details.

- More or less **materialistic** (through "goods production" and specific feedback about orientation of production). This directly impacts the quantity of stocks (with the possibility of having them so high that it could lead to waste).

- More or less **environmental** (through "environment" and "resource usage reduction"). Positioning oneself on these topics means positioning oneself relative to future generations, on the world we want to leave them.

- More or less **progressive** (through "fundamental research", "training" and specific needs expressed in each area of activity). All these directly impact the adaptability of the economic system.

- More or less **secured** (through "safety') with a possible shift toward a world where the police may feel too present.

The advantage of this comprehensive approach is that it allows everyone to position themselves on the society they wish, while being fully aware that any dissatisfaction shown in one area will automatically affect other areas. Eventually, there is no fundamentally good or bad choice (in some reasonable limits), but what is crucial is that it allows each individual to express an opinion that will impact society, thus eventually **allowing citizens to be collectively "in control".**

Another key point of the proposed model is that all human activities are pooled, i.e. funded by all. Any initiative, be it economic or social, is a risk, but this risk is borne by the entire community which, through the new democratic principles, has granted the decision-makers the power to take these initiatives.

This reflection leads to another key point: we must try to make the past investments as profitable as possible, by reusing anything that has been produced so far.

This is the case of all inventions, artistic creations, pieces of information and, in general, all digital assets that, once produced, are free of rights. We thus avoid any problem of piracy. And on the contrary, we can have reliable data regarding their usage. The already built infrastructures are rented to decision-makers with a value based on offer and demand to maximize their usage.

The last key point to mention in relation to this model is that it simplifies things in a very significant manner. It does not rely on complex financial mechanisms, based on growth rate, inflation, prime rate... There is simply a productive workforce, represented by a global budget available to be invested in full, to provide goods and services to share with all.

This will not prevent to have discussions on how the budget is allocated. But these are healthy and concrete discussions, not debates on artificial financial mechanisms.

Additional budget details

Crowd-funding mechanism

The collaborative model is based on the idea of raising some specific needs or issues, allocating some budget to each area of activity, and then allowing decision-makers to choose which specific solutions to implement.

But one could imagine allowing everyone to invest part of this budget, a quite small one, directly to specific solutions. This would cover specific needs, matching maybe a niche, which therefore cannot easily be identified and pooled, but which are nevertheless real. By doing so, we would find back the classic crowd-funding mechanisms, currently quite popular.

Local expenses

The investments corresponding to **local expenses**, is decided globally, but must then be split between each local area (region, department, city or village). We could split it equally, function of the number of citizens per local area, but it seems interesting to adjust it in order to balance the level of equipment between geographical areas. The idea is that each inhabited area continues to progress but all areas gradually tend, over the long term, to an equivalent level of equipment per citizen.

"Support" areas

Citizens express their wishes only on areas that directly affect them, i.e. provide goods and services they directly benefit. However, there are some **"support"** areas that do not fall into this category, as being less visible. Still they are essential and could in fact be useful to many different areas, like raw material production, office building, data center… We must therefore define a mechanism for setting the framework, and especially budget, of these areas.

The appropriate mechanism for this is simple and logical relative to the approach we have had so far: direct clients of these support areas must be in charge of defining this framework.

The idea is thus to identify these clients, name representatives, let them formalize the framework, collecting feedback from all. The corresponding budget is drawn on the budget of each area, proportionally to their corresponding expenses level. By defining the objectives and means for these areas, they make sure to have a fruitful and efficient activity in these areas, and reasonable prices, least their own activity be impacted. It's a real investment they do.

Participating to the framework definition

Democracy is viable only if the majority of those affected by a decision have the ability to speak knowingly. Various solutions can be applied.

First of all, we need well designed **forms**, that allow citizens to really express what they feel presently, in all areas: what are their wishes, their frustrations, the issues they face, their values...

We reach a **high level of representation** by letting citizens who do not want to vote be represented:
- Either by a particular person
- Or by a **profile mechanism**. When a citizen triggers this option, he first chooses a specific profile based on various social and cultural information such as age, gender, family status, occupation, religion, interests... then his or her vote will correspond automatically to the average vote of citizens matching this profile.
  For example, a retired person might say: I do not want to bother with voting, but rather than having a blank vote, I want my choice to be identical to the average vote of all retired persons who have voted.

We give all individuals the possibility to express themselves by making a systematic usage of **internet**.

We can also make available the **consequences of each positioning**. On each topic on which citizens are polled, the probable significant consequences of any modification compared to the previous results can be assessed in advance, from one year to another, and this information is made available to citizens.

It will be the representatives' role to interpret and formalize this information in a synthetic manner. Several interpretations are possible (all the representatives do not necessarily have the same point of view), the goal being that the representatives work together to put in light a handful of consensus. Eventually, the number of representatives supporting a point of view will be known and will help citizens identify interpretations with maximum support.

Some may be concerned about the ability for everyone to understand the information provided, and vote rationally. Is it reasonable to let everyone express themselves on questions that will impact the whole society?

First of all, as mentioned before, we simply ask people to mention how they feel towards the society they live in, what are their values, their frustrations and satisfactions, their fears... All this is real, and can easily be expressed.

Furthermore, we won't ask people to specify budget aspects directly, with numerical values, we will rather ask questions like "How much do you care about environmental aspects?" or "How safe do you feel?". It will be much simpler to answer, and the result can still easily be used to define final budgets.

We can also require voters to pass a basic examination, based on simple questions about the nature of economic and social framework they participate in defining through their votes. Only those people who succeeded in the examination get a "voting passport". Others will have to select someone or a specific profile to represent them, as described above.

We make sure this latter situation remains exceptional by having some training program at school explaining the whole collaborative system, providing details on the forms used when voting and the list of topics included in the vote.

Wages and incomes

Requirements

Let's now review how **wages** (what a company has to pay to employ someone) and **income** (what this person will receive eventually) are defined in the collaborative model.

Each worker has a value for the entire community and as mentioned before, wages are based on supply and demand, without minima (or only a low one). This is the best option to boost the labor market, assess training needs, encourage everyone to aim at positions on which there is strong demand and seek excellence in their job.

However, the consequence is that some wages may be very low, not giving the possibility to live decently. Also some people are not yet or no longer able to work, or temporarily disabled.

A collaborative society can only be a society with the moral obligation to support everyone. Some may go further, postulating that a fair society should be based on equal incomes for all, or at least a fair income, i.e. based on work duration and hardship. And thinking otherwise just increases social tensions and undermine society.

People in training (children and adult) is also something to take into account: providing an income for trained people is somehow logical as training serves the whole society. Doing so allows everyone to benefit from some training in full serenity, thus allowing decision-makers to stop obsolete activities in order to start new modern ones, thus eventually making sure society keeps innovating at a steady pace.

The solution to all this consists in setting a mechanism that readjusts income based on wages, situation and age, and allowing citizens to express themselves on the orientation they wish for this adjustment. This input will let us define the detailed corresponding parameters to be used.

My personal opinion is that the result of such a vote would lead to a factor of a few units between minimum and maximum incomes, letting everyone benefit from the motivation generated by high wages, without causing too important social tensions. But it will be citizen's full and only choice eventually.

Settings

The specific parameters supporting this mechanism are beyond the scope of this essay. However, one can imagine that they include at least:

- Either a universal income allocated to all without conditions (as is being discussed presently in some countries), Or a base income, also allocated to all, but depending on the category and age. The category is a tricky issue because the information has to be reliable. One could probably distinguish:
  - o Workers (people with a job),

- o Trained people:
    - Children and young students,
    - Adults in training
- o People without work and not in training, possibly with the possibility to distinguish:
    - Those no longer able to work (or not having a full capacity), for example children in infancy, elderly people, or people with an obvious handicap,
    - Those not wishing to work nor get trained (for whatever reason).
- The balancing parameters could be in example: minimum income, maximum income and a balancing factor. With a simple formula, these three parameters can let us rebalance low wages at the expense of higher wages, the balancing factor specifying how much everyone is affected. This is only an example, other parameters are possible.

Note that the economic model should easily offer low skilled positions (thus a priori with low wages) to all. But through balancing mechanisms, they can give a more interesting final income than just the basic income allocated to people not wanting to work.

Bonus

The teams that perform most in each area can also receive a premium. And part of this bonus will obviously be given to the decision-maker who granted the production team some mandate, thus some budget.

Citizens should be polled about this mechanism so that their wishes help define the precise budget share converted into premiums in each area.

Access to training

Access to training is made accordingly to a supply and demand mechanism. We can imagine awarding everyone with a quota specifically used to access training and earn some income. It would be allocated once at the beginning of schooling period, and available for the entire lifetime.

Everyone should then manage this quota at will to facilitate this access: long in the beginning then shorter thereafter, or short at the beginning with the option to take a new professional direction later on, or short but expensive training (because sought by many, thus *a priori* of higher quality).

Prices

Collaborative economy doesn't rely on sales revenue to function. The sales results are only used to evaluate the profitability of each solution, and thus the skill of each decision-maker and production team.

However all goods and services must be priced in order to effectively share them among citizens.

Today the price is based on various constraints, such as:
- Covering the manufacturing costs,
- Covering previous investment, such as those linked to R&D, new infrastructures, ...
- Getting the highest profit, leading to put unrealistically high prices, especially when competition is non-existent or weak,
- Including taxes,
- Taking into account scarcity.

In the collaborative model, we can only keep one of these constraints: scarcity. Thus, any price is expressed in terms of scarcity, and only in terms of scarcity. This is an efficient way to manage supply and demand. It has lots of virtues.

Especially prices can be dynamic and help maximize the use of services and sale of goods. The prices and their evolution can be managed by decision-makers, under the control of independent entities. But it is also possible to let independent entities manage this aspect entirely. The benefit is to let them define and apply best practices. There are probably advanced theories on this subject that exist or could be developed.

In a simplistic way, let's say that the **price of a product** can be first determined by comparing its quality relative to other similar products. It will then evolve according to supply and demand, which depend on delay before next delivery and the intrinsic quality of the product. In particular, the price of a perishable good must decrease as the expiry date approaches. The price of a product that becomes technically outdated or outmoded can also be decreased to get rid of existing stock.

The **price of a service** is initially fixed on the price of a similar service, and then changes according to how it becomes used:
-   If the service is underused, the price should decrease
-   If the service is overloaded, the price must increase

The ideal price is reached when the service is used at *almost* its maximum.

Fluctuations depending on the season or even during the day are quite possible, depending on how demand evolves.

The price of a good or service compared to other goods or services is full of **insights** for citizens and decision-makers. It allows a clear assessment of the skill of each economic structure offering these goods or services, and the scarcity of global offer, which can be used by citizens and decision-makers in many ways.

Decision-making processes

Introduction

Two main decision-making processes are used throughout the world presently:
- a vote based on majority (direct democracy),
- and the direct process, where a leader or manager in a hierarchical organization takes decisions directly.

The defaults of both are obvious.

The classic way of doing **direct democracy** (used essentially by citizens when naming their leaders, or by senators and deputies when validating laws or budgets, or inside boards of directors) is pretty shameful and inefficient, inherited from millenniums of fight for power: the majority imposing its decision onto the minority.

Hierarchical organizations (private or public) are useful at a small scale, when day to day decisions have to be taken in a quick way, but it's very risky for all decisions with high stakes, engaging high costs or having a long term impact. It's especially an open door to satisfying personal interests. Here also this type of organization is mostly a consequence of mankind's love for personal power.

These two processes don't really support the definition of democracy, a governance "by the people, for the people", and more precisely, "by **all** the people, for **all** the people". We need to come up with better mechanisms than the existing ones.

Several decision-making processes must be considered, adapted to each case. Let's specify the way each process works, and in which case each shall be used

Direct Democracy "polling"

This process is used to let **citizens define the economic and social framework**, through various forms established by the representatives. The principle is simple: each citizen expresses his wishes on one of the possible choices, and the result is an arithmetic average value (when possible, for example for wishes per area of activity, or solidarity and enrichment settings), or a percentage of vote for each proposed option.

Some of these choices are converted rather directly (to define budgets per area for example), others are targets that decision-makers must strive to achieve. They will thus serve in the evaluation process to measure the effect of each decision.

Overall, this is a good process as everybody's opinion is taken into account. It's not a question of skills, but only of polling people on present and wished society.

It will also be used by **first level representatives**, when they have to answer some polls. Here also average values will be used.

Improved Direct Democracy

This process will be used by **second level representatives**, for all the decisions they have to take (see the detailed "representatives section" further about the type of decisions they have to take).

As they may not work physically close to each other, we can imagine they use a Wikipedia-like process: everyone can propose an adjustment to the current organization, and all other representatives can position themselves on this adjustment.

The way to proceed to improve the process is not to vote by "yes" or "no", but rather let participants evaluate how satisfactory they perceive each proposal.

Let's illustrate this with an example, where a set of representatives have to position themselves on two options (one could correspond to the present situation, and the other one a new proposal).

The table below illustrates how satisfactory each representative evaluates each of these two options (between 0 and 100).

	Option 1	Option 2
Representative A	50	30
Representative B	60	80
Representative C	70	80
Representative D	50	70
Representative E	70	20
Global support	**300**	**280**

We see that a vote based on majority would lead to validate option 2, an option highly appreciated by three decision-makers but not at all appreciated by the other two. Instead, a **"collaborative" vote** will promote Option 1, overall a more satisfactory option.

We can even go further and take into account the **mean deviation** (based on the absolute value of the difference between the vote and the average vote). Let's illustrate this through another example.

	Option 1		Option 2	
	Support	Deviation	Support	Deviation
Representative A	50	10	40	20
Representative B	60	0	80	20
Representative C	70	10	80	20
Representative D	40	20	80	20
Representative E	80	20	20	40
Sum	**300**	**60**	**300**	**120**
Average Support and mean deviation	**60**	**12**	**60**	**24**
Final result	**48**		**36**	

Deviation of option 1 for Representative A is the absolute value of the difference between:
- the support of Representative A for this option: 50
- the average support for option 1 : 300/5 = 60

So it's $|50-60| = 10$.

Deviation of option 1 for Representative C is $|70-60|=10$.

We see that both options have the same average support (300), but if we take into account the mean deviation solution 1 is clearly better.

I feel this approach can really be a breakthrough in all decision-making process. It can be used in any group and any situation where a single decision has to be taken for the whole group while not caring too much about the skill of each participant. Underlying mathematics is extremely simple; small and simple mobile applications can be designed to help implement them practically.

Let's remark that some people may express themselves as they are used to, thus answering by a support of 100 for one option, and 0 for the other, leading us to fall back to the classic majority-based process.

But all people who evaluate things in good faith will start improving the process, and little by little, with appropriate training and as people see the benefits of the new process, new habits can be taken.

Let's note also that representatives do not aim at being reelected. They are simple people, with a short mandate. And the decisions they take do not have a direct impact on their day to day life, only on the decision-making process and framework related to one area. This should also lead them to evaluate each proposal in good faith.

« Competitive » process

This process applies when **several competing solutions can exist simultaneously**, the effects of which are all based on the same criteria.

This situation authorizes a simple process: every decision-maker has a budget, which is proportional to his or her power, and that he or she may invest, in an autonomous way. With it, he or she can deliver a mandate and part of this budget to an existing economic structure.

The evaluation is done by comparing the effect of each solution implemented versus the effects of each alternative. The decision-makers who financially supported the most effective solutions grow up in power, while the others diminish.

Remember that the ultimate goal of every decision is to match citizen's wishes. In the case of competitive solutions, we must distinguish several cases:

➔ When the goal is to produce **individual goods or services**, that is to say, the purchase of which is the result of an individual and voluntary act, then the sales results and operating costs will be used to assess the relevancy of each solution, like today. The goal of each decision-maker is simple: have the best profitability, expressed as the ratio between sales and operating costs. A high profitability is indeed something implicitly wished by all.

Let's specify a crucial point: we won't look at whether the costs are covered by the sales. These two notions are both expressed on a purely rarity basis, which is somehow logical (decision-maker uses rarity to produce some rarity), but the only way we use these data is to compare the relative profitability between each decision-maker. Said otherwise: in a given area, to which the citizens have allocated a budget, which decision-makers made the best use of the part of the budget they were entrusted with?

In example, a businessman can be more effective than another because he produces the same product than his competitors but in a cheaper way. Or because he produces a better product, in same quantity and for the same cost, thus having a higher demand and therefore, logically, a higher price and potentially higher profitability.

➜ When the purpose of the investment is **other than a purchasable product**, specific criteria must be specified. For example many companies could co-exist with the goal of reducing pollution in an area. The criterion will be the measure of the depollution, balanced against the operating cost.

This mechanism can be applied on most budget items.

➜ For new **infrastructures**, delivering new features (e.g. the manufacturing of a plant using a new technology to offer new type of TV sets), their rental price is a good indicator of their value. So comparing the profitability of different infrastructures, evaluated as the ratio between the total lease costs for several years vs. implementation cost would be an efficient way to proceed.

➜ All **creations** which, remember, are free of rights, will also require a specific model. This will be the relative use of each creation, balanced against the production cost, or it could be the profitability of solutions implemented, based on these creations.

For example all movies produced in a year could be compared using the number of times each one is viewed (whatever media is used), assuming that, being free of rights, we can obtain reliable information about these values.

Technological innovations in one area, such as a new manufacturing process of solar panels, can be evaluated by the use made of it or by the effective gain it brings (based on specific criteria) vs. the development cost. This 'profitability' is then to be compared with other similar solutions.

→ Let's note we can also set up a complementary mechanism to help decision-makers know if a project has enough potential, and ultimately ensure that only the most promising solutions are adopted: the idea is to identify a threshold of "profitability", this word must be taken in the broad sense "efficiency of solution vs. its cost", the efficiency being based on specific criteria, to be defined on a case by case basis, as described above. This threshold is evaluated and updated regularly in the light of past results. That is, in a simplified manner, the average profitability of all similar solutions implemented lately.

A solution has any interest only if it aims at a profitability above the threshold, thus providing a major indication about what profitability is expected for any new solution.

→ As a final remark, let's note that if no specific objective criterion can be found, we can revert to a subjective one, i.e. **a survey** specifically established and conducted by all representatives in the field.

These people have enough knowledge, skills and time to go enough in details and do a worthy and fair evaluation.

« Concerted » process

This process is used when **a single solution must be applied**. Heavier to implement, we'll use it especially when we have no other possibility, such as when establishing a law or a standard. Also this process can be used for projects whose stakes are high, such as projects requiring a huge investment, or projects related to some resource of high value (e.g. a tourist site or a high-tech factory). In this case the decision doesn't pertain to the budget to be used as it's defined through the framework defined by the citizens, and adjusted by the representatives (also if the solution concerns a specific resource, there is no concurrency on who will use it, so no rental cost for it). But the decision pertains to the precise content, i.e. a mandate or general strategy assigned to the economic structure in charge of the project, with the possibility to update its organization, appoint a new manager/representative...

Traditionally, these decisions are taken by senators, deputies or by a board of directors, and the decision-making process is a classic direct democracy process.

Like today, the decision-making process I recommend involves several decision-makers, to stimulate debate and possibly make several solutions appear. But the final decision shall not be made through a basic vote at the majority; instead it shall be made taking into account the skill of each decision-maker.

So we need to consider that each decision-maker is granted some decision-making power (a simple value) that measures his or her skill. And as a consequence we need an evaluation mechanism that enables us to grow up the best ones, i.e. the best visionaries, those who are able to correctly anticipate the effects of each solution.

The precise mechanism is actually very simple: we must first establish the **criterion that will measure the desired effect**, taking into account wishes expressed by the citizens. As before, it can be a criterion of profitability (sales vs. budget invested), or a specific criterion. It can be a weighted sum of several individual criteria. The important thing is that it must be expressed in such a way that the higher the value, the better.

Once this criterion is defined, each decision-maker specifies for each potential solution considered what will be, according to him, the expected effect. And his decision-making power is taken into account to assess the confidence that the community has in his own assessment. The option chosen eventually is the one that offers the hope for maximum effect.

For example, let's imagine two decision-makers A and B, and a decision to make with two options, 1 or 2. The sheet below illustrates how each decision-maker considers each option. The global support is based on a formula that takes into account the power of each decision-maker (40 and 70 respectively).

	Power	Vote Option 1	Weighted Support Option 1	Vote Option 2	Weighted Support Option 2
Decision-maker A	**40**	120	4 800 *(40 x 120)*	90	3 600 *(40 x 90)*
Decision-maker B	**70**	75	5 250	100	7 000
Global Support			**10 050**		**10 600**

We see that the decision retained eventually will be option 2.

After the solution is implemented, we can reevaluate the skill of each decision-maker based on the real effect measured. In the previous example, let's imagine the value used to assess the effect is eventually measured at 80. In this case, the appropriate calculations show that A's power will be slightly increased and B's power will be slightly decreased, because A's estimation for the adopted solution was closer than B's one.

Here also (as we did for the direct democracy process), we can improve the concerted process even more by taking into account the mean deviation, thus favoring decisions that avoid extreme divergences, as they represent a big risk (in this regard, option 2 is much better). And here also small and simple applications can be designed to help implement this process practically.

Furthermore, one can imagine that the decision-makers who have elaborated, suggested and supported the retained option can grow up more than the others. They could in example have a double assessment if it's positive, thus encouraging people to come up with new ideas.

This process leads to a **paradigm shift** in the approach of decision-makers: each decision-maker will aim at assessing in good faith the estimated effect of each proposition, even if it does not come from him or her. Eventually decision-makers who have the best chance to progress are not those who argue at all costs for their personal beliefs, but rather those who have the ability to listen to all parties and develop and support decisions capable to induce maximum effect, that is to say satisfy all people involved in a balanced way.

Additional ideas

Another decision-making process may be considered, called "**spread over**". It is an adaptation of the previous process, particularly applicable when multiple solutions are in debate, that is to say that the gap between the final assessments of two or more solutions is low. Although a single solution seems desirable, one can consider the implementation of multiple solutions but spread over different local areas, or spread over time, applied one after the other successively.

Logically, after some time, these experiments will provide enough information to decide the appropriate best solution, with maximum agreement. If it still doesn't meet consensus, one can also maintain the principle of keeping different solutions by region.

Such a process, especially implementing various solutions in multiple local areas at the same time, is also quite welcome when there is a risk that the real results are distorted by other side aspects, i.e. evolution of society that were unexpected. If this evolution affects all locations where the various solutions are experimented, then the best solution can still be identified.

Another difficulty can affect the "concerted" process, it occurs when no objective criterion appears clearly, i.e. a criterion that decision-makers can really evaluate in advance before taking a decision, and which can then be objectively measured after the retained solution has been developed.

In this case, we could revert to a subjective criterion, i.e. a criterion of "overall satisfaction" that will be measured by a survey conveyed among representatives. Though it's subjective, these people have time and skill to analyze more thoroughly the results compared to what was planned, and the potentially unexpected difficulties that may have occurred while the solution was tested.

Conclusion

As a conclusion to this whole section, we see that we have a panel of solutions, each adapted to a specific situation, and all of them being better than the classic decision-making processes.

Note that among the set of decisions taken today at the state level, we tipped many of them on a direct democratic polling process, including all those related to economic, budgetary issues.

These represent a majority of decisions, and often a source of tension between citizens, and also between the different political parties.

One last note: a social decision quite always has some economic component. For example a law generally requires some budget to be implemented. Or a decision may include financial compensation for those impacted negatively. Only those options with sufficient financial support can be retained. The easiest solution is to consider the decision-making power of a decision-maker is both political (ability to support a solution in a concerted process) and economical (ability to use part of the budget allocated to the area).

Decision-makers

Decision-makers are mostly appointed by representatives. **New decision-makers** can thus integrate the system (usually with a reduced decision-making power) if they convince representatives, through their skills or through an innovative project for example. Logically, less competent ones also lose their capacity to participate. So there is a natural flow that will take place, to make sure we always have efficient people, with new generations coming in, carrying renewed visions.

Furthermore, any person working in a given area automatically accumulates some decision-making power with time, in this area. This capacity increases with position and results. Thus experienced people may adventure themselves in financing a project, possibly a project they will conduct themselves. They may be technical experts, or very creative people, or managers used to make decisions in their positions. By partnering with others, they may collectively have enough decision-making power to start their project. If they succeed compared to other competitors, they will then get more funds from the community.

Similarly, a group of people can of course initiate an activity, using its own personal resources.

In both cases, the goal is to develop an activity that proves to be relevant, thus gaining attention from a decision-maker (who can then finance the activity) or representatives (who can then grant some decision-making power, thus a budget, allowing to finance the activity in the long term).

The only constraint is to respect the price policy, based on supply and demand, so that the activity can be properly assessed relative to competitors.

Representatives and administrators

In each area, two levels of representative are needed, as well as administrators in charge of the operational stuff. Let's specify things in detail.

First level representatives

The first level of representatives in an area is made of all the non-paid volunteers, under condition that they have a good knowledge of the area. A form, pretty basic, will be established by the second-level representatives to make this selection.

Their role is:
- To tune the framework:
  - ○ Clarify the budget break out, to the highest level of detail.
  - ○ Clarify what is expected for the area, by tracing citizens' feedback or specific wishes with respect to the area. It can for example be defects on an industrial product, or a wish for a new functionality.
- To respond to surveys prepared by the second level representatives (in example to assess the results of some decisions).
- To participate in forums on area-related discussions.

Second level representatives

The **second level of representatives** is smaller. They are picked randomly, among volunteers who meet the following conditions:
- Having been a first level representative for a few years
- And having passed a test validating that they have the knowledge and skills required for this role.

They will have a short term contract (e.g. three years) and will be paid for this activity (not necessarily full-time). They must be in adequate numbers: not too many, in order not to represent an excessive cost, but numerous enough, in order to be sure that their contribution is globally relevant, and to establish a real and close relationship between citizens and decision-makers.

Representatives operate through an improved direct democracy process on all their tasks. Internet operation is essential, with the possibility of occasional physical encounters.

Their role is to oversee the area, track down all dysfunctions and frustrations, and take the necessary decisions pertaining to the decision-making process to make the area progress in the right direction. They therefore have a complementary role to decision-makers.

Their tasks include the following:
- Launch any study or analysis required to evaluate the situation properly in their area.
- Define the voting passports for all citizens.
- Define the recruitment forms for first and second level representatives.

- Formalize the forms that will let citizens give their feedback on society, thus eventually defining the economic and social framework.
- Define some production standards (see the next chapter).
- Identify and support new decision-makers.
- Be privileged interlocutors for decision-makers by communicating on details that help define the framework, anticipating reactions to proposed decisions.
- Provide adequate highlights to allow citizens to express themselves knowingly.
- In regards with each specific decision:
  o Define the type of decision-making process (competitive or concerted, or spread over)
  o Formalize if necessary the effect that will be estimated for each solution implemented, and ensure that these effects are evaluated in due time.
- Adjust (to some degree) evaluation of decision-makers, taking into account any unpredictable events that may have occurred.
- Finally, they can exercise a veto only on high stakes decisions, provided that a large majority of representatives (for example at least 80%) wish to exercise this right. This should be exceptional.

All in all, citizens, representatives and decision-makers are well advised to work in a collaborative manner.

Administrators

The representatives rely on **administrators** in each area to help them with the practical aspects.

Their tasks are:

- To manage decision-making process ('concerted' one especially) from a practical point of view.
- To manage financial aspects.
- To convey defined surveys, also from an operational point of view.
- To manage all information flows transparently.
- To ensure access to information.
- To validate claims made by anyone during debates, thus ensuring information and debate quality.

System efficiency

Lots of people will be concerned by the efficiency of the collaborative economy. Some may confound it with communism. Many think only liberalism is worth considering, and whatever the cost for some people, it's eventually beneficial to mankind as a whole.

I've detailed in the previous chapters some key aspects that will make sure collaborative economy is efficient (through regular evaluation of decision-makers and bonuses, among other things) and serves mankind (as economy is oriented towards expressed needs). But we can increase efficiency through several other aspects. And these evolutions are made possible in each area of society, especially thanks to forsaking private sphere.

Competition and collaboration

As in the current economic system, the proposed model works all the better that we have a lot of competition: a healthy **competition** in all fields, quite close to what we can have in sports, source of dynamism and progress, and this is something representatives will keep in mind.

This being said, it also allows **transparency, information and innovation sharing, and synergy**. The idea is that once a decision-maker (or a team) has innovated and advanced a domain, he or she is valued because of this, but this innovation is then made public so that all who wish can freely benefit from it, thus allowing all to go one step further.

All economic and social data will be accessible to all, thus helping all people involved in the decision-making process take better decisions. New tools made to visualize economic activity or increase access to information could also be designed to help them in their work. Data availability will also help administrators check what representatives and decision-makers say publicly.

Economic ecosystem

Furthermore, the designed model, based on a continually renewed investment and a guaranteed minimum income for all, allows the entire system to be flexible and scalable. The system will be dynamic, adapting, restructuring itself to gain in efficiency.

And to support this flexibility and competition, it would be wise to **limit the size of economic structures**: instead of heavy entities, powerful but static, we must aim at a system of smaller, flexible and dynamic 'cells', in collaboration or competition one with each other.

The large hierarchical organizations that exist today are actually a collection of operational services managed by an upper management who defines their mandates and practices, ensures the flow of goods and information between all of them, checks their performance and updates the overall structure as needed.

This type of organization can be completely reshaped by considering that each service is independent but works with other services for its own interest, exploiting the goods, information or practices they produce. Each cell knows it must be efficient, have a collaborative spirit and be transparent on its activity and progress. Those that do not perform sufficiently well in all these aspects quickly disappear.

To quote the adage "small is beautiful", a limited size offers many advantages: it is particularly easy to create and close cells, or have cells compete one with each other. It is also easy to evaluate a cell's efficiency.

The fate of a cell is in the hands of decision-makers who entrust it with a production mandate. These are therefore demanding on economic structures and only those that are convincing enough have a chance to carry on.

Conversely, a cell is not linked to a decision-maker in an unwavering way: a decision-maker creates a cell and entrust it with a mandate for a few years, but then this structure may decide to collaborate with another decision-maker, receive another mandate, and thus an operating budget. This establishes a balance in power, and avoids excessive hierarchical organizations.

The entire system can make us think of an **ecosystem** where each cell is a living organism, in constant interaction with its environment, either collaboratively, or competitively fighting for the mandates proposed by decision-makers. Each cell is an economic agent which must be responsive to survive.

Production standards

Sometimes it is useful to standardize certain economic practices, and sometimes it is better to unleash creativity, even though the situation becomes chaotic for a while. Natural cycles can thus appear.

Representatives can play a very useful role regarding this, enlivening the debate about possible standards, and formalizing them or not, depending on circumstances.

It will be more effective than today, where standards often appear as a result of economic struggles and marketing campaigns, and not always based on criteria of quality for the consumers.

Organization & motivation

We can increase the efficiency of the whole system by **improving the organization within cells**.

A cell is like a small civilian society, in which all employees of the cell, from bottom to top of the internal hierarchy, have a common goal: having a performing cell while ensuring satisfactory working conditions. All employees want an efficient organization but also be more in control, making sure the decisions are taken "**by the employees, for the employees**".

We should thus adapt the classic organization, using the collaborative concepts previously described.

Of course the organization must remain essentially hierarchical. This guarantees that the day to day decisions are taken quickly, and thus the cell's operations are fluid and responsive. However there are a lot of key decisions where we should use a better decision-making process. These are especially:

- acceptance of production mandates,
- validation of budgetary and salary guidelines,
- evolution of the organizational chart.

To improve the situation, we should have, in addition to the usual hierarchy:

- **A board of directors**, that takes the key decisions of the cell through a "concerted" decision-making process, each director having some decision-making power.

- **Representatives**, chosen at random among all volunteers with enough support from employees (e.g. 20%) and not already sitting on the board of directors. Their main function is to:
  - Poll employees regarding their problems and expectations of the cell, and synthesize this information to make it accessible to all.
  - Update the decision-making power of each member of the board of directors based on his / her ability to achieve the objectives defined by the employees.

We thus have a virtuous circle: employees elect their representatives, who adjust the power of the directors in the board, themselves updating the hierarchy, which manages the employees on a daily basis.

Other organizations are possible, especially for the smallest cells. In example, the directors could be directly appointed each year by employees, through an improved democracy mode. The number of votes received by a director defines his/her decision-making power.

These types of organization will clearly enable the cell to gain in quality on key decisions, and thus on all its operations. It should also eliminate a large part of the frustration that everyone can experience in their job. It gives at last the possibility for all employees to express themselves and have some weight, i.e. some control, on the decisions taken by the structure they work in. This should increase the motivation of all employees, and thus the way everyone gets involved in their job. A collaborative cell fully becomes a collective adventure.

We can also increase individual **motivation** in a different manner: indeed, it may be related to higher salaries and bonuses but it can also go through strong reorientation capacity (based on training budget), and an increased public recognition of individual and collective contributions in all areas.

Human nature

Some will say that the proposed model is utopian, because **incompatible with human nature**, and in particular our desire for power. Some think that any major change is possible only when the very nature of mankind has changed. I think instead that this component was perfectly integrated into the collaborative model.

For a long time, violence and physical dominance determined the social structure of society. Then as mankind became more civilized, a new form of society appeared where police and justice helped channel this instinct, preventing everyone to express it easily, thus letting other facets of the human personality drive society. Yet this capacity remains in us, in our genes, our inner nature.

It can be the same for our desire for power, the ability to dominate others or use the system for personal gain. This is a fundamental component of human nature, shaping up our present civilization. Yet we can equip our society with institutions that reduce the negative impact of this aspect significantly, keeping it at bay as much as possible. The proposed institutions were designed to achieve this, it was one of the pillars used for their design.

Of course some will attempt to subvert the system for their own benefit; of course crime will not disappear. Nevertheless, I think these new institutions are strong enough to resist such behaviors.

Instead, transparency and disappearance of private economy will enable community to rely on a highly computerized system that will cross all public financial data: production, sales, wages, incomes... Such a system would enhance fight against criminality a lot, and avoid many abuses that can't be detected today.

Freedom and property

The abandonment of the liberal economic model will be a matter of concern for many people. Let's see how the collaborative model is positioned in the area of **individual freedoms**, compared to more liberal models, or less liberal ones.

Like the liberal model, and unlike the communist model, the collaborative model promotes individual freedoms in the sense that it respects everyone's ability to manage one's own life, and be the most independent of external constraints. The existing constraints are social rules collectively decided, especially to guarantee life in society and everyone's security. They may be more or less developed, but they are always the result, not of a state, but of an orientation decided by citizens as a whole.

And that's the big difference, the great strength of the model: it gives control to citizens in all fields, it promotes freedom of speech and individual expression of all. This is a great tool to prevent what we see today in the Western model: despite our so-called democratic civilization, we feel the overwhelming power of a minority - the rich people, the world of finance, parties and politicians, lobbies... - directing all human activities and influencing legislation in depth. Eventually a few impose their will, thus constraints, to the greatest number.

In this sense the collaborative model is much more liberal than the current model. It would be a breath of fresh air for many, finally free of the weight of the powerful ones, and able to take control of their destiny.

On the side of private property, even if the collaborative model requires that the community has ownership of all means of production, it stands out from the communist model because it recognizes private property, that is to say the freedom to own property, and consume at will.

Fierce defenders of the liberal model will of course criticize the limitations on individual enrichment capacity and the transmission of inheritance. Here also, these can be very flexible or very constrained, but in all cases they are the expression of popular will. The system is not to be criticized because of that.

These same advocates will criticize the non-ownership of productive assets and the inability to sell the fruits of one's labor at any price. These are indeed strong constraints.

However, all means of production are made available to all decision-makers, who can operate them in an independent way once they have a legitimate right to use them. And if they perform, they can keep this use over the years and gain appropriate bonuses.

Furthermore, all those who wish to undertake projects, innovate and contribute to the progress of society, compete with others, mark their time, and fulfill themselves through this (and have a personal gain, as much as a certain renown) have definitely the possibility to do so. It will even be much simpler today with representatives listening to any new idea, workers getting automatic decision-making power as they progress, and budget dedicated to innovation.

We keep all the strengths of the liberal model, without its excesses. In the end the weak constraints on individual liberties seem a small price to pay to give control of its destiny to the greatest number.

Implementation

We may wonder how to implement such a model, from a practical point of view. If citizens in a country wanted to do so, how would the transition takes place?

This is a key question, as it is crucial for a society of several million people, all accustomed to a certain standard of living, to maintain this standard as much as possible during the transition, under penalty of a destructive social chaos.

Also, it would be of course too risky to switch to such a new model, without experimenting it before, and adjusting any details.

Such local or partial experiments would also contribute to spread these ideas a lot, and convince an even larger amount of people.

Transition steps

Let's talk first about the transition.

We can take benefit from one of the strengths of the proposed model: it's a marvelous tool to make a society evolve in a given direction, wished by citizens, but it can start from any situation.

So we can consider that all social rules (laws, norms…) and all current human activities (with current budgets) actually correspond to a particular orientation of the new collaborative model, as if it were the current choice of the citizens, and then let society evolve little by little towards a more desired orientation.

With this in mind, let's review the various steps through which such a transition would take place.

At first, we do not change the system, but start preparing the transition. We must recruit representatives in each area, and to do so, we first need to elaborate the appropriate passports / forms that will help select them. To achieve this, we pick randomly among the most skilled people working in each area, and ask them to elaborate these passports. Their contribution is made public so as to make sure they have a collaborative approach.

Once these representatives are appointed, in each area, they will perform an audit of their field: identify decision-makers, the cells they finance and the budget available to them. They will also define the type of decision-making process to be used in each case. When competition is possible, and stakes are not too high, favor the competitive process. In other cases, favor the concerted process and make sure there are several decision-makers in charge.

If there are no existing decision-makers dedicated to an area or not enough, representatives must appoint new ones, selecting among the volunteers with enough background in each area. Each will receive a fraction of the decision-making power allocated for this area.

Other representatives must be appointed to have a more global approach, and especially define the current overall budget breakout for each area. They will also evaluate the current enrichment and solidarity settings. These become the official parameters of the new model.

The existing economic data already available shall prove much useful to finalize this first step.

For sure, it won't be that easy to complete this step, but it's achievable provided we allocate enough time and means to do it.

Secondly, we switch to the new financial model without changing current operations. The only difference is in the financial flows: the financial revenues of the business activities of a company no longer go directly to that company. But every decision-maker / cell receives from the community the budget they had so far, with the same mandate to continue the current activity. Similarly, all workers are now paid by the community with their current wages.

All infrastructures become the property of the community, but we make them available for free to the economic structures using them presently.

The big organizations must progressively be split in multiple more autonomous cells, competing or collaborating.

Digital goods become free, patents become accessible to all.

In each area, the representatives will also establish the forms letting citizens express their wishes, so that these can, year by year, gradually reorient society.

Thirdly, we let social and economic activity unfold and evolve according to the new model, and we let decision-makers change society to match citizens' wishes. We also let the prices evolve in accordance with supply and demand, without floor value, to maximize the use of services and make a wise use of infrastructures.

A key objective will be to restore activity for all unemployed people. For this, we rely on the mechanisms identified, i.e. the removal of minimum wages, a universal basic income, and a mechanism to rebalance low wages.

Meanwhile, we end purely financial activities (grants, banks of investment, stock exchange...).

Note that it would also be wise to reconsider all marketing activities: of course we must highlight the new features, and strengths of each new product, but it must be done in a more global context, with the supervision of representatives by area, in order to focus all marketing activities on one valid goal: informing consumers wisely, with comparative information, giving a good overview of all existing solutions, with their respective strengths and weaknesses.

Finally, let's note that the collaborative system can be applied to a country or group of countries, while coexisting with other systems in other countries. We just need to formalize a currency and exchange rates. All currencies obtained by exporting goods become an internal resource to the nation, which each decision-maker can use (still through a supply and demand mechanism).

Short term implementation

Partial experiments

Partial experiments of the model are possible.

As seen above, any organized structure may abandon a purely hierarchical organization and switch to a more collaborative model, enabling a good collaboration between decision-makers and members of the structure.

Any organization can also switch to a model based on external representatives, who establish a good link between the organization and its customers.

Extending the concept, we could in example imagine implementing most of the practices previously described in **a state department**, like in example education or transportation (equivalent to an activity area). There is already a budget defined for such area, people working in this area are already paid by state… So it's "just" a matter of:

- having citizens contribute actively to defining the economic and / or social framework for this department,
- having independent decision-makers,
- introducing more competition,
- having representatives...

The minister (or secretary of state) would essentially be in charge of an effective implementation of the new collaborative practices, and defining the budget for that department.

Cooperative label

Another possibility exists, also viable in the short term. It's a solution that could be applied easily and quickly, and would make people sensitive to some of the concepts developed in this model.

The idea is to create a kind of **"Cooperative" label** for goods or services produced by companies that follow some "collaborative" principles. Such a label could rely on the following criteria:

- **Transparency**: for each product, allow to consult (via a QR code for example) a lot of details related to this product, such as:
    - Details related to the price, including:
        - Cost of suppliers
        - Employees wages
        - Preliminary investment required to make this product (design, infrastructures…)
        - Tax and other similar costs
        - Margin
    - Detailed explanation of product composition
    - Any useful information about how the product was made
    - Origin of raw materials
    - Any information regarding the company making the product, especially the way the margin is used

- **Relationship with customers**: this will evaluate the quality of the collaboration between citizens and the company delivering these goods or services:
  - o Bronze: the company has a survey form accessible to clients and managed by an independent organism, and the overall results are made public.
  - o Silver: same as bronze, plus the independent organism in charge of the survey is proactive, i.e. canvasses a panel of volunteers to have reliable and thorough information (both on positive and negative aspects).
  - o Gold: same as silver, plus the company publishes the actions decided to take into account the survey's results, and these are checked by the independent organism.

Conclusion

What are the odds are for such a model to see the light? And what may influence these?

As mentioned in the introduction, we are little in control of our destiny, and that is an obstacle to any significant changes. We all feel that existing institutions are somehow "locked", unmovable.

Yet I feel things start evolving. Lots of people are weary and upset by the issues I raised in introduction. Many realize these are linked to our institutions, and some start thinking of out-of-the-box solutions, trying to identify what is most likely to be the '**next system**'.

Major evolution often results from unbearable tension. We can assume that current institutions will at some point in a near future generate extreme tension, revealing obvious weaknesses of these institutions and the need to develop something utterly new. The advent of robotic in example could be the cause of extreme social tensions, when businessmen have at their disposal a workforce more effective and much cheaper than the current one. And this may well occur during this century. Thinking of viable alternative is thus in the air, but it's also essential!

I've tried to use a format that gives the best chance for this essay to be understood and spread. Especially, I've had in mind to keep a good balance between a short enough essay, readable in one shot, and enough details to see the practical implementation.

Still, it may be difficult for anyone to elaborate a mental image of such a collaborative society, imagine what it would really be like, on a daily basis, seeing both the whole picture and interactions between all its parts. Even though the initial ideas are simple, their consequences are huge. It takes time (and probably several readings) to really give shape to this vision.

The logical approach I've followed may prove helpful: starting with the strengths and weaknesses of our current society to establish the pillars on which any new model must rest, and from there define new democratic principles and eventually new institutions, first as an overview, then in more details.

These details are important because too often, when a person or a party offers a radically new proposal, it boils down to vague intentions, general ideas, not allowing us to see what it would look like concretely.

Also, please note these details and the underlying principles are the fruit of a lot of trial and error, over a few years. Giving the model its present shape was achieved by stressing the fundamental principles, by seeing how to implement them effectively through new institutions.

I've also tried to answer some expected criticisms, about human nature or forsaking the liberal model, for example.

Still, it's quite likely there is even better to put in light, some aspects clearly suffer from a lack of details. Eventually, only **experimentation** will validate this model, or advance it to something even better, or supplement it with appropriate details before generalizing it. I've provided several tracks to go in this direction.

As a final word, I would like to express how comforting it is to me to imagine such a society, to have laid down this model, to know that it exists: it's a bright window opening on a new world, more serene, more efficient, more social, avoiding most of the problems affecting our society today while being viable over time.

The path to it will be long for sure, assuredly decades, maybe the whole century... Still, I feel in my heart it could become real.

If you feel the same or even if you find this proposal has any potential to nourish reflection, then please share it with everyone you know. Only by disseminating new ideas can a new model of society become real: a new proposal that, little by little, becomes so obvious, such an absolute necessity that it's able to overthrow all obstacles.

Thank you for your reading and your support!